Earnest's Search

by Judy Mills
illustrated by Len Ebert

Core Decodable 51

McGraw Hill Education

Bothell, WA • Chicago, IL • Columbus, OH • New York, NY

MHEonline.com

Send all inquiries to:
McGraw-Hill Education
8787 Orion Place
Columbus, OH 43240

ISBN: 978-0-02-145214-9
MHID: 0-02-145214-8

Printed in Canada.

9 10 11 12 KOD 24

Earnest learned to swim.
Earnest liked to swim.

Earnest liked to search under the water.

Earnest swam and searched.
Earnest searched for shells.

Earnest kept up his search.

Did Earnest get any shells?

Earnest got a shell from the water.
What is in it?

It is a pearl!

Earnest got a shell and a pearl!